Charlie's Little Tramp

By Jeremy Geltzer

Also by Jeremy Geltzer
Behind the Scenes: A Child's Guide to Film History
Oscar Micheaux: A Self-Made Man
Race Films
Latino Hollywood
Cinema Censorship & the Law

Published by the Hollywood Press
hollywood-press.com
First Edition December 2013
Second Edition, January 2016

Charlie Chaplin mugging for the camera during the making
of his third film, *Kid Auto Races at Venice* (1914).

For inspiration I thank my wife Heather Donaldson Geltzer.

This is for my son Jackson.

Charlie's Little Tramp

Cinematographer Frank Williams, Charlie Chaplin and director Henry "Pathe" Lehrman on the set of *Kid Auto Races at Venice* (1914)

Winter rain fell lightly on the South London street. Even in the drizzle, the factory's smokestacks puffed thick clouds of black soot into the gray sky. The streets were busy with people shopping. Horse-drawn carts delivered wooden crates of green apples and red potatoes.

One man hustled through the crowd politely excusing himself as he passed washer women and fruit sellers. The man was wearing a fancy jacket and tie, but if you looked closely, you'd see that his jacket was threadbear and patched at the elbows. His tie was only a torn piece of red fabric that he had folded nicely. His hat had been crushed and carefully smoothed out.

"Excuse me, guv'ner," he said with a British accent as he patted a mule that wore a yellow straw hat. "Pardon me, kind sir."

He arrived at a red brick building. A broken sign hung above the door. The sign read: "Children's Factory."

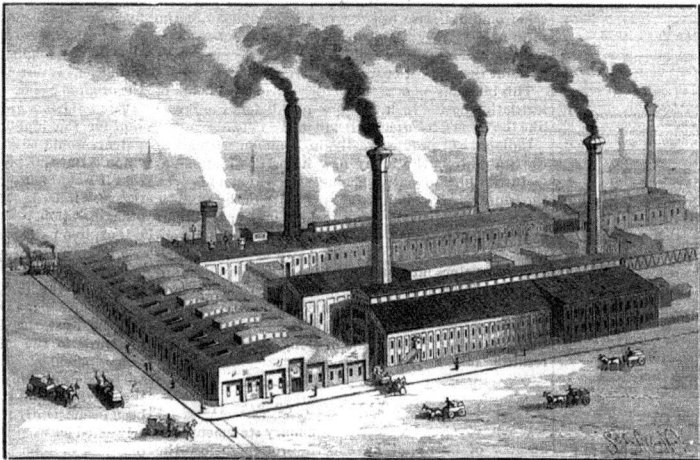

GENERAL VIEW OF MANUFACTORY.

"Hey Mister, you can't stand there. We got deliveries coming in," a thick lipped guard scolded.

"Top of the morning to you, mate. I'm just waiting for my young friend. He'll be getting off a long shift."

"Understood, but it's my job to keep that walkway clear."

"Is it OK if I stand over there?"

"Why don't you wait in the alley and I'll look the other way." The guard turned his back to Max.

Max stood in the alleyway as the rain misted down. Soon he heard the sound of workers leaving the factory. Grime-crusted children came out through the factory gates as the nighttime shift ended. In the distance, a bell tower rang the early morning hour.

One boy passed through the gates with a funny little walk, as if his toes pointed outwards.

Boys in a Cigar Factory, August 1908
Courtesy of the National Archives and Records Administration,
Records of the Department of Commerce and Labor,
Children's Bureau

"Psst," said the man in the alley. "Psst, Charlie."

The boy looked up and said, "Hello Max! It's good to see you. What are you doing in the alley? Did you do something wrong?"

"No, no, not at all. I was waiting for you. Here, I brought you something." Max reached into a coat pocket and unfolded a thin cheesecloth. "Thought you might be hungry after a long shift." He handed Charlie a slice of wet bologna. One bite had been taken. "Sorry, I got hungry," Max smiled.

"Oh thank you. I'm starving. They don't give us meal breaks and I've been working ten hours straight."

"You're a good boy, Charlie. You're a hard worker. Someday you'll get what's coming to you."

"All I want is a good meal and a dry roof over my head. I'd be happy for just that, I would."

"Ah, simple pleasures are the sweetest. Come on, you can catch up on some sleep at my flat. It isn't much, but the roof doesn't leak and you'll be out of the rain."

"Warm and dry sounds good to me right now. Thanks, Max."

"One more thing—I unloaded a truck for a man today. The gentleman couldn't pay me with money.

Children factory workers in London in the 1880s.

It seems that no one has any money these days, but he gave me two tickets to a show. See?" He held out two colorful cardboard tickets.

Charlie's face broke into a big smile. "Karno's Troupe! I've always wanted to see them. They're the best act in London."

"You deserve it. The tickets are for tomorrow night. We'll dry you off, get you fed and rested and then have some good laughs."

The next day, Max and Charlie put on their best clothes. They weren't much better than what they were already wearing.

"I've got some newspaper to fill that hole in your shoe, Charlie."

"And look, Max, these pants almost fit!" Charlie pulled up some plaid trousers. "I'll just need a length of rope for a belt."

Charlie Chaplin in 1909

"That's as good as done, I have a good strong rope holding the window open here." Max hadn't told Charlie that he once knew the owner of the troupe. "We want to look good tonight," he said as he adjusted a limp carnation in his lapel.

Max and Charlie arrived at the tent early.   As they walked to their seats they heard a voice.

"Well spank my bottom and powder my wig if it isn't good old Max!"

"Is that Fred Karno, you old dog?"

They gave each other a hearty handshake. Then they stepped into a giant bear hug. "Where have you been all these long years?" Mr. Karno turned to Charlie and pointed at Max saying, "this fine fellow was one of my best pantomimers."

Max smiled warmly and said, "Mais oui, but Fred practically invented the cream-pie-in-the-face gag."

Young Charlie in 1909

"So what gives, Max? What have you been up to?"

"Oh, I've been doing a little bit of this, a little bit of that. Making ends meet and keeping out of trouble." Max hadn't told Charlie that years ago, he had been the most famous clown in the show. Audiences loved Max from Paris to Portugal. They cried "Bravo!" for his antics from Berlin to Belgium. But then one day, Max Linder just dropped out of sight.

"Fred, I want you to meet my friend Charlie. Charlie, this is Fred Karno of Karno's Traveling Troupe."

"It's good to meet you kid," Mr. Karno grabbed Charlie's hand roughly and almost shook Charlie out of his shoes. As he spoke, he kept on shaking Charlie's hand. "Good to meet you. I saw you come in. I like the way you walk. You have a funny walk."

"He's a good kid, Fred. He's a hard worker."

FRED KARNO'S
LONDON Company
Alf Reeves
"NIGHT IN ENGLISH MUSIC HALL"

"Enjoy the show Max. Maybe let's talk afterwards. The troupe's heading to America and I might need one more player." Glancing down at Max's tickets Fred twisted his face in a funny expression. "Hey, why are you sitting all the way up there in the cheap seats? I'll not have a friend of mine sit in the bleachers. You two sit down here in the front row. And come see me after the show."

"Thank you sir," Charlie tipped his hat.

Mr. Karno laughed. "That's good kid. Funny. You're good. Keep up that walk and great hat tip—it's hilarious. Enjoy the show."

Karno Company performing "Mumming Birds" in 1903.

Charlie Chaplin on tour with Fred Karno's comic troupe. An advertisement from 1913 (right), and with the troupe posing somewhere in Montana, 1912 (below).

Empress

WHERE EVERYBODY GOES

Three Shows Daily, 3, 8 and 9.30 p.m.—Mats. 10 to 25c.   Evgs. 10 to 35c

CHAS. CHAPLIN

As He Is

THEY'RE BACK AGAIN AFTER MAKING MILLIONS LAUGH

KARNO'S

LONDON COMEDIANS

With CHARLES CHAPLIN and a company of fourteen, in "A NIGHT IN A LONDON CLUB"

CHAS. CHAPLIN

As "Archibald"

The Noted Character Comedian	Musical Comedy's Cleverest Pair	Remarkable Human Salamanders
Geo. F. Hall	Brierre & King	The Nagyfys

ROLAND WEST ANNOUNCES THE NEW FROLICSOME FARCE

"THE TAMER" With MABEL FLORENCE and BERESFORD LOVETT

A FEATURE FILM AND THE EMPRESS ORCHESTRA

"America—can you believe I'm going to America with Karno's Troupe?" Charlie didn't have much to pack.

"Don't count your chickens before they hatch, kiddo. You still have to make it across the ocean and that tramp steamer hardly looks seaworthy." Inside, Max was very happy for his young friend, but he missed the days when he traveled the world and made people laugh. "Naw, don't worry. You have great things in your future."

Charlie Chaplin and his friend Max Linder.

Karno's ship didn't look so good. It was old and dirty and burped up sickly puffs of gray smoke. Charlie was a little scared as he walked aboard on the rickety gangplank. He didn't know when he'd see London again. But then again, he didn't have much to leave behind.

With trembling steps, Charlie boarded the rusty boat. He had never been on a ship and didn't like the way the water swayed. He felt a bit sick. He could hardly stand up.

"You're not looking so good. Are you feeling a little green around the gills?" A boy about Charlie's age smiled at him. "Let me guess. It's your first time at sea. Pleased to meet you, my name is Stan. I have a hammock set up below the deck. You can use it."

Charlie and Stanley became good friends. Stan's wide smile cheered Charlie up during the long seasick days and nights as the ship chugged across the Atlantic Ocean.

Finally one day Stan woke Charlie by shaking his shoulder. "Quick, come up front Charlie."

Good friends: Stan Laurel (left) and Charlie Chaplin (right), around 1910.

Charlie tried to smile. "I'm still feeling a bit ill, Stan. I've been seasick for days."

"Trust me. Come on!" Stan led Charlie to the bow of the boat. "See? Look at her. It's the Statue of Liberty!" The tall green lady towered in front of them as they headed toward the twinkling lights of New York City.

The boat pulled into the harbor and Karno's Troupe was soon set up on a small stage off Broadway. Charlie and Stan roomed together in the Bowery. It was dirty and crowded and reminded them of London. But when they hopped aboard the shiny brass trolley that took them uptown to the theater in Times Square, they were transported to another world.

Karno's show went well but Mr. Karno was never satisfied. The comedy could always be funnier, he said. "I don't just want laughs. I want the audience to fall in love with your characters." The seats were almost full each night but Karno wanted a full house. He wanted standing room only. He wanted sold out signs. Charlie did tricks, slapstick and pantomime. He sang, danced and joked. The crowds loved it. Everyone loved it except for old man Karno.

One night Karno came in and told the actors they had to be the funniest they had ever been. "We have some very important people in the audience tonight." It's all Karno would say.

MOVING PICTURE STARS

CHARLES CHAPLIN

Charlie Chaplin in 1910 (right) and
with Fred Karno's Comedians, tour-
ing Spokane, WA in 1910 (below),
Charlie is standing to the far left.

FRED KARNO'S LONDON
PANTOMIME CO.

RGE A. DEANE & CO.

MME. FIFI RONAY'S
TRAINED TOY POODL

PONDER & EARWA

WILL OAKLAND

Empre

Chaplin's first American app

That night Stan and Charlie and the rest of the troupe sang, danced, joked, flipped, pranked, jeered and mugged. It was their funniest show ever. Still, Mr. Karno looked sad when he came backstage.

"Stan," Karno's voice sounded very tired, "tell Charlie he'll have a visitor in the dressing rooms tonight."

Charlie was packing up backstage when Stan told him. "A visitor," Charlie wondered aloud, "I wonder who it could be? I wish I had some better clothes." He was still wearing clown pants, thick suspenders and an undershirt. He hadn't washed off all his pancake make-up. A white smudge ran across his upper lip. Just then there was a knock at the door. Stan walked over and opened it.

A very small woman in an enormous fur coat and feather boa stood outside eating an ice cream sundae from a tall glass.

Stanley looked at her with a puzzled expression. Then he said, "And you're name is..."

The Karno company on tour in the USA. Charles Chaplin is on the right.

"Oh good grief, you don't know who I am? I'm famous." She popped a knotted cherry stem out of her mouth and looked at it. Then she tossed it over her shoulder. "Famous in America anyways. OK, you kids are from England, so's maybe you don't know."

She didn't wait for the boys to respond. "My name is Mabel. Mabel Normand. And I'm a star—in the flickers. The movies, moving pictures, comedies. People from all over know me and love my funny movies."

Mabel finished her sundae and set the empty glass down. "The job's a peach. I just came back here to say to Charlie, I like you're funny little accent. Of course no one'll hear it because we're making silent movies, but you got a good face. And a funny walk."

Mabel Normand

MABEL NORMAND

MACK SENNETT ... RAYMOND HITCHCOCK

The STOLEN MAGIC

A MACK SENNETT COMEDY

PHOTOPLAY
MAGAZINE

The World's
Leading
Moving Picture
Magazine

August
20 Cents

"Anybody Can Swim!"

BUY WAR
SAVINGS
STAMPS

"Want To Be a Star!"

"Thank you, Miss Mabel."

"Oh quit it with that Miss, stuff, you're making me blush." Mabel reached into her fur coat. She pulled out a silver case and pressed a button. It flipped open and out slid a card. She held it toward Charlie. "Go ahead and take one."

Charlie reached forward and pulled the white card from the shiny case. It said:

Mabel Normand
Movie Star
Keystone Studios
Hollywood
U.S.A.

"If you're ever out in California, kid, look me up. We're always looking for fresh faces. Comedy is a dirty business. Your friend too. He's got a nice smile." With a flourish of her feather boa she turned and marched out. The two boys sat silently watching the doorway. Finally Stan told Charlie to wash off his clown make up because it'll give a rash if you keep it on too long.

The BRADSTREET of FILMDOM

Wid's DAILY

The RECOGNIZED AUTHORITY

Sunday, September 15, 1918   Vol. V No. 128   Price 25 Cents

Mabel Normand

That night at their hotel Charlie and Stan lay in their bunk beds. Charlie was in the top bunk. He stared at the ceiling. Stan was in the bottom bunk. He looked at the shape that Charlie's slim body made along the mattress. Outside a siren howled in the New York night. They could hear horses pulling the milk trucks down the street.

"So..." said Charlie.

"Sew...buttons," offered Stan.

They sat in silence and listened to the night.

"Well..." said Charlie.

"Well...water," Stan said helpfully.

"Would you quit it Stanley! I'm trying to have a serious conversation with you."

"Say something serious then!"

"Fine! What do you think about going to California?"

"I think that's a crazy question." "Why?"

"What's in California?" Stan nudged the mattress with his foot.

"That lady, Miss Mabel, said we'd be good in the movie business."

"Charlie, she was nuts. Did you see the way she ate that ice cream? Everybody knows you should let the ice cream melt and then spoon the melty. Secondly, we're getting to be darn good clowns. Did you hear the people laugh tonight? Movies are just flickering lights. Black and white. No sound. But most importantly, California is a thousand miles away. We don't know anybody and we don't know anything. Karno is heading back to London next week. We can return to merry old England, save up some money and head to California in a few years if the movies are still around."

"I can't wait a few years, Stan."

"What are you saying, Charlie?"

"I don't have anything in England to go back to. I like America. I like the people and the trolleys and the streets. In London, I was just a poor kid with a dirty factory job. In America I can be whoever I want to be. I can start over. I can be a millionaire."
"You've been eating too much of Mabel's sundae."

"I mean it Stan. I'm not going back. I'm going to find Mabel in California."

"Suit yourself, buddy. I'll miss you. But when you're famous, can I borrow your act?"

"Of course you can, Stanley. But in the meantime you can use our piano moving skit."

Stan Laurel and Oliver Hardy's Academy Award Winning piano moving stunt in *The Music Box* (1932).

"That always cracks the audience up. I'll miss you old chap."

"And I'll miss you, old bean."

The next week, Mr. Karno wasn't surprised to find Charlie missing as the boat headed back to London. "He was a good kid. I wish him all the luck," Karno thought as the old boat floated out to sea and back toward England. Karno stood at the stern watching Lady Liberty grow smaller in the distance.

Charlie was headed in the opposite direction. He hopped a railroad and was chugging west. The locomotive left New York and passed through green Pennsylvania. Then the landscape became flat as they sped through the Midwest: Ohio, Indiana, and Illinois. He got off in Chicago and spent a few days in the Windy City.

Charlie couldn't wait to continue his westward journey. The Midwest gave way to the wide-open

Kansas. Soon the snow-capped Rocky Mountains looked down on little Charlie. He shivered in the chilly air.

The train climbed up the mountains and sped through the desert. Charlie couldn't believe how big and wonderful America was. He missed Stan and wished he could have shared the experience of seeing the world with his friend. The train crossed the California state line and continued heading toward the sunset. When they reached the coast the golden sun was dipping into the Pacific Ocean.

Charlie had never seen a palm tree before. The long skinny trunk that curved up to a tuft of green fronds made him smile. He had come a long way—from the coal dust of a London sweat-shop to the ocean breeze and swaying palms of the West Coast.

"I'm going to like it here," Charlie thought to himself as he dozed off in the yellow sands of Santa Monica's beach under the orange sunset.

"Hey buddy boy, you can't sleep here." A policeman kicked sand over Charlie's face. "Hey, what are you, a little tramp? You can't sleep on a public beach, kiddo." Charlie woke up spitting sand out of this mouth. The morning sun was bright and warm.

"I'm sorry, sir." Charlie brushed himself off. "Could you point me in the right direction to go?" He unfolded Mabel's card from his pocket and presented it to the officer.

"Oh, an actor is you? I should have guessed. I should run you down to the jail. We have too many actors in town all ready. So, you're a friend of Mabel? That gal is nothing but trouble. But today's your lucky day, kiddo. You know why?"

"No sir. Why?"

"Because Mack Sennett and the Keystone Kops are shooting a movie on the pier right now."

"Who are they?"

"You *are* really green, kiddo. A newbie. You just off the boat from somewhere?"

"Why, yes a train actually. A boat first then—"

"Button it. Mack Sennett is the King of Comedy. He's Mabel's boss. He runs Keystone Movie Studios. And the Keystone Kops are a ragtag group that's always causing trouble but they sure make some funny movies. Look over there. You see all that commotion?"

"Yes, sir I was wondering—"

"I'm not asking you a question. All that commotion on the pier is the Keystone Kops doing their thing."

"What's their thing?"

"Causing trouble of course. They make mischief, mayhem and monkey business. They cause chaos, confusion and commotion. You get the idea. Come on, I'll walk you over there, at least it'll get you off of my hands. You'll be their problem."

"Thank you, sir."

"That isn't a compliment."

Mack Sennett's fun factory churned out many Keystone Kops comedies between 1913-1915, including *The Bangville Police* (1913).

"Since you obviously don't know nothing, let me point them out to you. See that big guy over there, that's Fatty Arbuckle. He's the most famous one, a real crackerjack. This one here, he's Slim Summerville," the policeman pointed at a tall gangly man standing next to Fatty. "Slim is a champion pie thrower—can hit any mark on the first toss. They say he's saved Sennett a million bucks with his great aim."

A silly looking police paddy wagon swerved up. A little man with crossed eyes tumbled out of the driver's seat. "That's Ben Turpin. He's got his eyes insured for a million bucks in case they come uncrossed! And look over there. That pint sized fellow with a big walrus mustache, that's old Chester Conklin."

The mismatched Kops ran around in circles chasing each other. They kicked each other in the butt. One pulled on another's mustache. A pie hit a bumbling kop in the face. One Kop was too fat, another too tall and a third was too skinny. One skittered on bowlegs, another did a funny Russian dance, kicking his feet out and crossing his arms. They looked ridiculous.

"Hey," said Charlie scratching his head, "how do you know so much about the Keystone Kops?"

The Keystone Kops

Mack Sennett, Ford Sterling and Roscoe "Fatty" Arbuckle.

"Because I'm one of 'em." The policeman did a somersault. "Chief Teeheezel at your service. Woo Hoo!" He made a silly face, stuck out his tongue and poked Charlie in the stomach with his billy club. "The name's Ford Sterling. I've worked with Mack and Mabel for years. Any friend of Mabel's is a friend of ours. I wasn't in this scene, so I wandered around the beach and found you. That right there is Mack Sennett, the King of Comedy." Chief Teeheezel, otherwise known as Ford Sterling pointed out a big, broad shouldered man who was shouting at the bumbling Kops through a megaphone.

Mack Sennett's voice boomed through the cardboard cone and when he laughed it sounded like thunder. He wore a yellow boater hat with a red, white and blue ribbon. Or rather, he held the hat in one hand and beat it against his leg as he laughed at the shenanigans of the Keystone Kops.

"Alright, alright, cut! Cut already!" When Mack Sennett barked orders, everyone stopped in their tracks. "We filmed some funny scenes here today. Let's head back to the studio for the grand finale."

"Ahem, Mr. Sennett?" Chief Teeheezel approached the King of Comedy.

"Ford, what happened to you?"

"I wasn't in this scene."

"I don't pay you to take walks on the beach. I pay you to be funny. When the camera's rolling, I want you pratfalling. Make me laugh." Mack plopped down on a folding chair that said "Sennett" across the back.

"I found a friend of Mabel's. This kid. His name is...state your name, kid!"

Charlie stumbled forward. "My name is Charles. Sir. Mr. Sennett. Charles Chaplin."

"Oh." Mack pushed his hat to the back of his head. "The British clown, from New York. Mabel told me all about you. She says you're funny. I need funny. And I trust Mabel. Fine, you'll shoot a scene tomorrow. Where are you staying?"

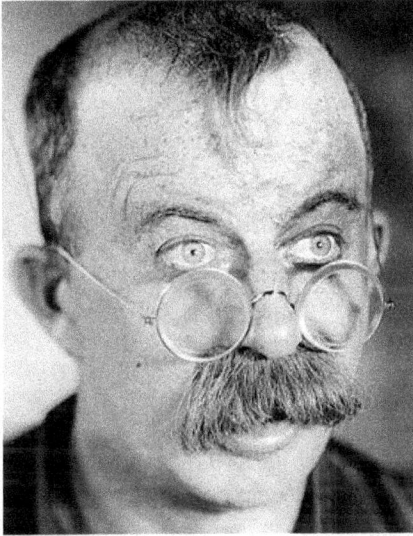
Chester Conklin

Charlie looked at his feet.

"I found him sleeping on the beach, Boss." Ford piped up.

"That won't do. That won't do at all. We'll make him a bed at the studio. Chester!"

The little man with a giant mustache turned around.

"Yeah boss?"

Mack continued in his booming baritone voice. "Chester, I want you to take care of our new friend. OK folks, that's a wrap for today, we're finished filming here. Close it up, clean up your mess. Ben, why don't you mop up those custard pies so no one slips on them. Charlie, you can pile into the paddy wagon with the rest of them. Next stop, Keystone Studios."

That night Charlie lay awake. Chester had made him a bed in the wardrobe and props closet. Funny looking hats hung on hooks along one wall. Jackets and clown pants were heaped in a pile. There were bicycles, tricycles and unicycles. There were canes, umbrellas and pogo sticks. Many of the props were broken and taped together.

Chester had thrown a burlap sack over a plank of splintery wood and put a horse blanket on top of that. Charlie's bed wasn't the most comfortable but he wasn't worried—he had finally made it to a movie studio. Cozy or not, he had come halfway around the world and was ready to start a new life. His heart was racing but as the night got later his eyelids became heavier. Soon he was asleep.

"Come on, come on, kid! Wakey wakey. Rise and shine!" Chester's face was so close that his walrus mustache scratched Charlie's cheek.

"What time is it?" Charlie said groggily.

CONKLIN

"Time to get your funny on! Let's go."

Charlie stepped out of the prop room scratching his behind with one hand. He was still half asleep, but the Keystone Kops were moving at full frantic speed. They ran around and made a lot of noise but didn't seem to get much done until Mr. Sennett barked orders through his megaphone.

Through all the commotion, on the other side of the room Charlie saw her—Mabel.

Trying to cross that room was almost impossible. Everywhere Charlie tried to step, a Kop was ready to trip him or poke him or raspberry his cheek. Finally Charlie made it to Mabel. She was eating a huge slice of chocolate birthday cake.

"Hey good morning, kiddo. Glad to see you made it. I hear you met the boys."

"Hi Mabel. Yes I did. Are you eating birthday cake for breakfast?"

"I'm a movie star, I can do whatever I want! Watch this!" She tossed a banana peel into the action. Almost immediately Slim Summerville came loping by on his long legs. He slipped on the peel and fell on his butt. After sitting there for a second, he popped up and went on his way. "See?" Mabel said.

"Wow. That was funny." Charlie said.

"You're funny too, Charlie. That's why you're here. But remember that you have your own type of humor. Don't let these guys boss you around."

"Settle down. Settle down folks." When Mack roared through his megaphone everyone stopped in their tracks. "Enough warm-ing up. We got to get to work." Then Mack set his megaphone down and turned to Charlie. "Charlie, you won't be in the scene this morning. You just sit and watch and see how it's done. Remember that we're making silent films. No talking, right?"

Mack Sennett directing a scene.

"Oh you can talk," snapped Mabel. "You can talk, yell, scream and laugh."

"Yeah, but the people won't hear you. That's why we call them silent films." Mack smiled. "There's sound all right. There's always music when they're watching the movies. A piano player playing but no talking. It's not like the stage. You think you can get it?"

"I'll try my best sir," said Charlie. "Is there a script?"

"Script, heck!" Mack grabbed his hat with a big bear paw of a hand. "We make it up as we go along. But remember that we're telling a story without words. Use your eyes. Use your face. Use your body. You got that funny walk down already. Think about it. Sit and watch this morning and then after lunch, you're on. Got it?"

Ben Turpin

"Why are you going to use him?" Ben Turpin, the cross-eyed Kop piped up. He was looking in the wrong direction. "He's not funny looking. Look at him. He don't make me laugh. He don't even make me snicker."

"He looks OK to me." Fatty said.

"I'm not talking to you...Fatty," spat Ben.

"Please don't call me Fatty. I'm just big boned. Call me Roscoe." Fatty stuck out his lower lip and pouted like a big baby.

Ben Turpin was getting angrier and angrier. And the angrier he got, the more his eyes crossed. "This new kid is a dud, I tell you. I know these things!"

Chief Teeheezel sounded up. "Well, he isn't as funny looking as you, that's for sure. You have one ugly mug, Ben. This kid's kind of cute."

"My face is my fortune!" Ben looked like he was ready to jump out of his skin. "Go ahead and laugh but that's why I make $3000 a week! This kid is plain vanilla. A dime a dozen."

Mack nodded to Slim, his custard pie-throwing champion, as if to say, "OK let him have it." Slim cocked one long, lanky arm way back until his shoulder cracked. He squinted one eye to take aim. He balanced a custard pie in his wide flat palm. Then he launched it.

The pie whizzed through the air. It flew across the room and hit its mark. Whipped cream splattered all over Ben's red face. The cross-eyed Kop did a somersault in the air and landed on his butt. Everyone laughed.

"Listen, Ben. I don't need to know if you like the new kid or not. Mabel says he's funny. Mabel says he's got what it takes. And Mabel's got an eye for talent. So we're going to give him a chance." Mack was done with the fun and games and ready to start working. "Now Ben, get up and I want you to mop up this mess before we start shooting. Oh, and Slim—"

"Yeah boss?"

"Nice shot."

All morning Charlie watched the Kops work their slapstick comedy. Fatty and Slim played off each other. Big Chief Teeheezel and little Chester Conklin played off each other. Mabel was the darling and Ben was the wild one. Each one was bursting with energy but it was Mack Sennett who focused them. With his megaphone in hand Mack directed their whirlwind of comedy into a story.

Finally, after a morning of crazy antics the crew stopped for lunch. The Kops didn't stop, though. All through lunch they threw food at each other, putting sandwiches down their pants and gargling soda pop.

Charlie sat with Mabel and Chester. Their end of the table was much quieter.

Mabel & Charlie in *Tillie's Punctured Romance* (1914)

"Mack is a great mentor Charlie," Mabel was spooning down a banana split. "He may be a little rough but he can make you be your funniest. He says comedy is all about movement. That's why we're always chasing each other, see? I always thought your little walk was funny and different. Make sure that Mack sees your walk."

Just then Mack bellowed, "Half hour is up! I don't pay you to eat. Stand by and get ready to start up again!" Then, leaning towards Charlie, Mack spoke in a warmer and quieter voice. "Kiddo, you're on after lunch. Why don't you go back to the prop room and get a costume together. Chester, help the kid out."

In the prop room Charlie was surrounded by hats, coats, pants and so much other stuff that it made his head spin. He pulled a pair of old black pants off a hook and tried them on. They were too loose. He pulled a worn coat off a hanger and tried it on. It was too tight. None of the shoes fit him. They were all too big.

Chester burst into the room. "You're not ready yet? Come on Charlie, you can't keep Mack waiting. He don't like to wait. He likes things fast-fast-fast."

"I don't know what to put on."

"You look great kid. Your pants are too big, your coat is too small, and your shoes are ridiculous. It's perfect. You're almost ready. You need a hat." Charlie pulled a brown derby off a hook. It fit him just right.

He found a flimsy walking stick. "This bamboo cane is nice and it can protect me in a pie fight."

"Now you're thinking kid." Chester stroked his long walrus mustache. "You're almost ready, you're just missing something."

"Places everyone!" Mack hollered through his megaphone. His voice was even louder than before. "What's taking that kid so long? Someone go in and get the new guy. What am I, paying you to stand around? Come on! Don't make me wait, people."

"Hmm, still missing something," Chester repeated. "I know what!" He picked up a grease pencil and drew a toothbrush-shaped mustache on Charlie's upper lip. "I got a big mustache, so maybe it's funny if you have a little mustache. Right?"

"I think it's perfect Chester. Thank you!" And with that Charlie turned and walked his little waddling walk out of the prop closet and into a studio filled with Mack Sennett and the Keystone Kops.

Everyone became quiet all at once. They were all looking at Charlie. Mabel was the first to say anything. She snapped a **bubble gum bubble** and shouted, "Charlie you look great!"

"Enough standing around. Make me some funny," Mack roared, "Action!" The camera rolled. Charlie twitched his little mustache and leaned on his flimsy bamboo cane, then he walked out with his funny little walk. All the Kops—except Ben, who was still angry—laughed until they split the stitches in their uniforms.

"CHARLIE"

On that day in February 1914, Charlie Chaplin's Little Tramp was born. His first film was called *Mabel's Strange Predicament*. A few days later, Charlie squeezed back into the paddy wagon and rode back to the beach where Chief Teeheezel woke him up. This time Charlie appeared in a short movie called *Kid Auto Races at Venice Beach*.

Mabel was still a huge star. She made the world's first full-length comedy movie, called *Tillie's Punctured Romance*. Mack and Mabel made sure that Charlie had a good part in the movie.

Fatty found a new skinny man. The new kid had a stone face and glassy eyes. His name was Buster. Buster could take a pratfall like nobody else. Bit that's another story--as a matter of fact, it might be the next story! Much later on—almost 40 years later—Buster and Charlie would become friends and act together in a film called *Limelight*, but that's a tale for another time.

Slim always had the best pie-throwing arm in the business but he also made some serious films. He acted in one of the greatest anti-war films of all time called *All Quiet on the Western Front*. The picture won an Academy Award for the Best Picture of 1930.

Cross-eyed Ben Turpin started as a comedian and janitor. He was always the one to clean up after the pie fights. He became a big star because of his funny face and his daredevil pratfalls. He mostly retired from making movies in 1924 and used his money to buy apartment buildings around Los Angeles. Since he loved saving money he also was the building's janitor. Ben made his last movie in 1940

SLIM SUMMERVILLE
appearing in Universal pictures

and—you guessed it—he played a janitor, cleaning up other comedian's messes.

Good old Chester Conklin remained a friend to Charlie. Charlie never forgot the man who put the finishing touch on the Little Tramp. Even as Charlie became a bigger star, he kept Chester on his payroll year-round. He was always a friend when Charlie needed him.

As the Little Tramp, Charlie became the most famous movie star in the world. Everyone from Los Angeles to London, from Malibu to Moscow and from Venice Beach to Venice, Italy recognized his funny little walk. But in addition to starring in his movies, Charlie also started to write the stories and directed the films. He even composed the music and wrote songs.

In 1915, Charlie made a movie called *The Tramp* and everyone fell in love with the little guy. In 1916, he made *The Rink* and showed off his roller skating skills. In 1917, he recreated his old London neighborhood and showed everyone how he moved from a dead end street to *Easy Street*.

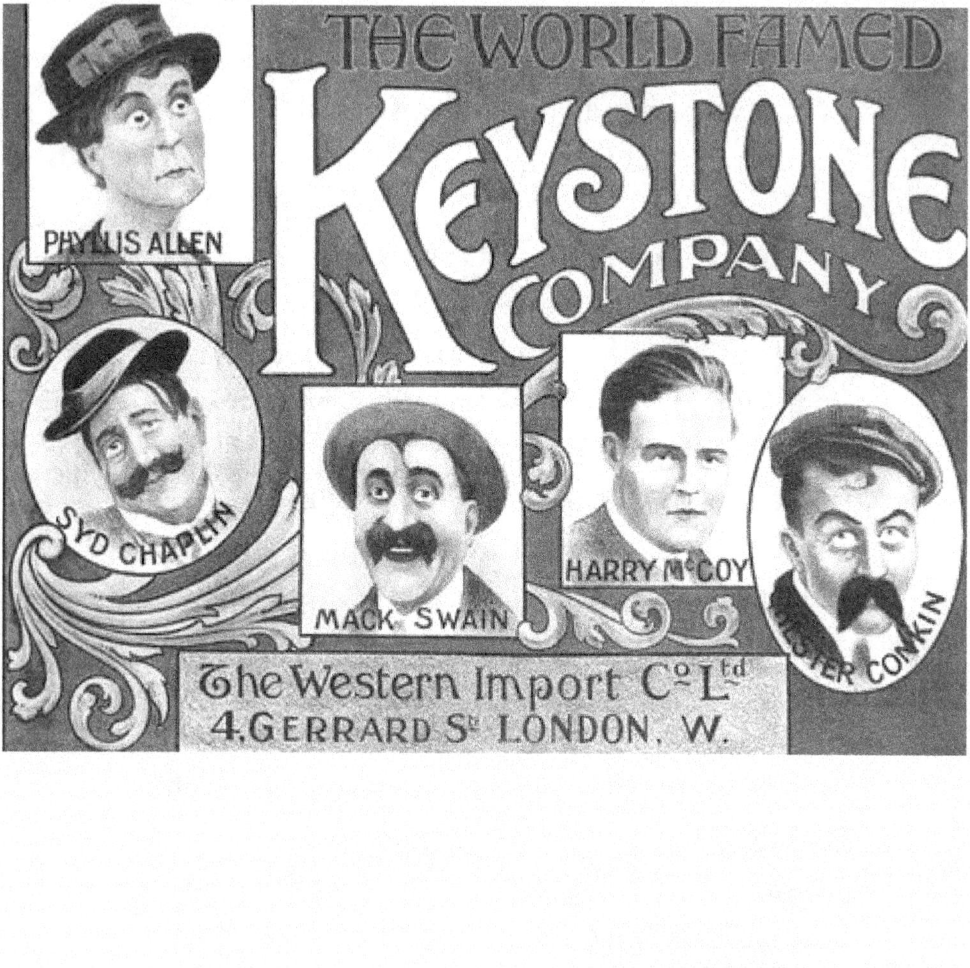
THE WORLD FAMED
KEYSTONE
COMPANY
PHYLLIS ALLEN
SYD CHAPLIN
MACK SWAIN
HARRY McCOY
The Western Import Co. Ltd.
4, GERRARD St. LONDON, W.

Mabel starred in *The Nickel-Hopper* (1926) with Oliver Hardy replacing Fatty Arbuckle (above); Charlie appeared with Chester in *Dough and Dynamite* (1914), and with Mabel in *Mabel's Married Life* (1914).

Charlie Chaplin and Jackie
Coogan in *The Kid* (1921)

Finally in 1921, Charlie told a story that followed closely to his real life "with a smile and perhaps with a tear." It was called *The Kid*. Charlie played a poor man, a tramp, living in ramshackle rundown house. In the film he finds an orphan boy and raises him as his son. Even though they don't have two pennies to rub together they have each other. It was the story of Charlie's life with Max.

Except in the movie the orphan boy discovers that his mother is really a millionaire. The tramp and the boy go to live happily ever after with her in her mansion. The movie was called *The Kid*. Around the world everyone fell in love with the kid, the tramp and Charlie. In real life, Charlie went on to become richer and more famous than he ever could imagine was possible. It shows you how important hard work, a sunny outlook on life and a funny walk can be.

Charlie became the biggest movie star in the world. Still, he never forgot where he came from. He even dedicated one of his films to his old buddy: "For the unique Max, the great master, his student Charles Chaplin."

And Stanley?

A couple years later, Stan Laurel made it to California and found a funny partner

Stan Laurel and Oliver Hardy

of his own named Oliver Hardy. Stan and Ollie started making movies together in the 1920s and became one of the best-loved comedy teams. In 1932, Laurel and Hardy's *The Music Box* won an Academy Award for Best Short Picture of the year. Stan and Ollie weren't just an on screen duo. They were also best friends. They made movies together for 30 years and when Ollie became too old to perform Stanley quit also because he couldn't bear to make people laugh without his partner.

Max, Stanley, Ollie, Chester, Mack, Mabel, Fatty, Slim, Ben and Buster made audiences split their sides with laughter in the days of silent film. But Charlie was the biggest star of them all. When silent films faded, many of these great comedians also went their own way. They may have been gone, but they weren't forgotten. You should try watching the Keystone Kops, Stan & Ollie or the Little Tramp— they're still just as funny a hundred years later!

Before he discovered the little tramp, Charlie Chaplin
made a living in films like *Making a Living* (1914).

Work and play in
Mack Sennet's fun
factory at Keystone
studios: *Tango
Tangles* (1914),
above and *Work*
(1915), below.

Tillie's Punctured Romance (1914) was the first ever-feature length American comedy (top); *Getting Acquainted* (1914), left, and *Twenty Minutes of Love* (1914), right.

HIMALAYA FILM C^{IE}

PRÉSENTE

CHARLIE
CHAPLIN

DANS

GARÇON DE CAFÉ

Série Record Pictures INC

DISTRIBUTEUR
LES PRODUCTIONS RÉUNIES
Anc^s Etab^{ts} FERNAND WEILL
9 B^d des FILLES DU CALVAIRE.
PARIS

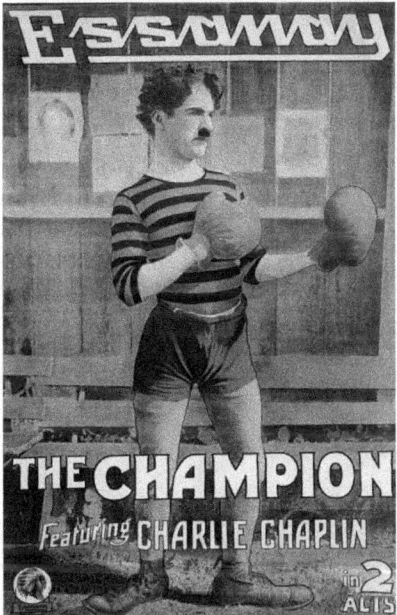

Charlie Chaplin in *The Tramp (1914)*

The Films of Charlie Chaplin

Films made for Keystone Studios
Mabel's Strange Predicament (1914)
Making a Living (1914)
Kid Auto Races at Venice (1914)
A Thief Catcher (1914)
Between Showers (1914)
A Film Johnnie (1914)
Tango Tangles (1914)
His Favorite Pastime (1914)
Cruel, Cruel Love (1914)
The Star Boarder (1914)
Mabel at the Wheel (1914)
Twenty Minutes of Love (1914)
Caught in a Cabaret (1914)
Caught in the Rain (1914)
A Busy Day (1914)
The Fatal Mallet (1914)
Her Friend the Bandit (1914)
The Knockout (1914)
Mabel's Busy Day (1914)
Mabel's Married Life (1914)
Laughing Gas (1914)
The Property Man (1914)
The Face on the Bar Room Floor (1914)
Recreation (1914)
The Masquerader (1914)
His New Profession (1914)

The Rounders (1914)
The New Janitor (1914)
Those Love Pangs (1914)
Dough and Dynamite (1914)
Gentlemen of Nerve (1914)
Musical Tramp (1914)
His Trysting Place (1914)
Tillie's Punctured Romance (1914)
Getting Acquainted (1914)
His Prehistoric Past (1914)

Films made for Essanay Studios
His New Job (1915)
A Night Out (1915)
The Champion (1915)
In the Park (1915)
A Jitney Elopement (1915)
The Tramp (1915)
By the Sea (1915)
Work (1915)
A Woman (1915)
The Bank (1915)
Shanghaied (1915)
A Night in the Show (1915)
Burlesque on Carmen (1915)
Police (1916)
Triple Trouble (1918)

The Films of Charlie Chaplin

Films made for Mutual Film Corp.
The Floorwalker (1916)
The Fireman (1916)
The Vagabond (1916)
One A.M. (1916)
The Count (1916)
The Pawnshop (1916)
Behind the Screen (1916)
The Rink (1916)
Easy Street (1917)
The Cure (1917)
The Immigrant (1917)
The Convict (1917)
The Adventurer (1917)

Films made for First National Pictures
A Dog's Life (1918)
The Bond (1918)
Shoulder Arms (1918)
Sunnyside (1919)
A Day's Pleasure (1919)
The Kid (1921)
The Idle Class (1921)
Pay Day (1922)
The Pilgrim (1923)

Films made for United Artists
A Woman of Paris (1923)
The Gold Rush (1925)
The Circus (1928)
City Lights (1931)
Modern Times (1936)
The Great Dictator (1940)
Monsieur Verdoux (1947)
Limelight (1952)

Later productions
A King in New York (1957)
A Countess from Hong Kong (1967)

Charlie's friends on film

Selected films of Mabel Normand
The Water Nymph (1911)
Mabel's Adventures (1912)
The Speed Kings (1913)
Mabel's Strange Predicament (1914)
Mabel at the Wheel (1914)
Mabel's Busy Day (1914)
Mabel's Married Life (1914)
Mabel's New Job (1914)
Tillie's Punctured Romance (1914)
Mabel and Fatty's Wash Day (1915)
Mabel and Fatty's Simple Life (1915)
Mabel and Fatty's Married Life (1915)
Mabel Lost and Won (1915)
Mickey (1918)
Oh, Mabel Behave (1922)
Suzanna (1923)
The Extra Girl (1923)
The Nickel-Hopper (1926)

Selected films of the Keystone Kops
The Bangville Police (1913)
Hide and Seek (1913)
Making a Living (1914)
In the Clutches of the Gang (1914)
The Noise of Bombs (1914)
Love, Loot and Crash (1915)
Love, Speed and Thrills (1915)

Selected films of Slim Summerville
All Quiet on the Western Front (1930)

Selected films of Roscoe "Fatty" Arbuckle
Fatty Joins the Force (1913)
Mabel's New Hero (1913)
A Bath House Beauty (1914)
The Rounders (1914)
The Knockout (1914)
Miss Fatty's Seaside Lovers (1915)
Fatty's Plucky Pup (1915)
Fatty's Faithful Fido (1915)
A Creampuff Romance (1917)
The Butcher Boy (1917)
The Cook (1918)
Leap Year (1921)
Buzzin' Around (1933)

Selected films of Laurel and Hardy
We Faw Down (1928)
Berth Marks (1929)
Brats (1930)
The Music Box (1932)
County Hospital (1932)
Sons of the Desert (1933)
Fra Diavolo (1933)
Babes in Toyland (1934)
Way Out West (1937)
Block-Heads (1938)
The Flying Deuces (1939)
A Chump at Oxford (1940)
Saps at Sea (1940)
Air Raid Wardens (1943)

Conclusion

Wallace Worsley directing Rhea Mitchell in Social Ambition (1918)

The lights go down. The curtains open. An image flickers to life on screen as we enter another world for two hours.

In this new world superheroes can defend the Earth from intergalactic and mutant villains. In this screen world a femme fatale can control a man with one smoldering pouty glance.   In this fantasy world comedians can drive a car off a cliff and walk away unharmed.

We love the movies because they can transport us to thrilling and glamorous dream lands.   The movies show us stories that can change our lives— or at least escape for a short time.

But stories behind the screen can be equally dramatic. The men, women, boys, and girls that made the movies can provide inspiring stories of success. Talents like Charlie Chaplin, Greta Garbo and Oscar Micheaux struggled to create a better life. With unwavering will power they made their dreams a reality—and they became screen legends. By reading their stories we can remind ourselves to never give up on our dreams and aspirations no matter how far away they may seem.

In the movies, anything is possible.

The End